EMPOWER "U" WORKBOOK

Part One: Building Your Self-Worth

EMPOWER "U" WORKBOOK

Part One: Building Your Self-Worth

ANN MARIE KAPPEL, MBA, Ph.D

Unless otherwise indicated all scriptural quotations are
taken from the King James Version of the Bible.

Empower "U" Workbook
Part One: Building Your Self-Worth
Copyright © 2016
Ann Marie Kappel, MBA, Ph.D

Printed in the United States of America

Library of Congress – Catalogued in Publication Data

ISBN 13: 978-0997784534
ISBN-10: 0997784539

Published by:
Jabez Books Writers' Agency
(A Division of Clark's Consultant Group)
www.clarksconsultantgroup.com

Jabez Books

1. Self-esteem 2. Personal Development 3. Self-Discovery

Table of Contents

Are You Motivated to Win?

"Your life today is the result of your attitudes and choices in the past. Your life tomorrow will be the result of your attitudes and the choice you make today."

Author unknown

PART ONE

Building Your Self-Worth

CHAPTER 1

DO YOU KNOW YOUR WORTH?

had the opportunity to speak at an event and while I was socializing a woman approached me. During our conversation, I asked her about her profession and she began to tell me. I then said to her, *"That is interesting, and I imagine it must be time-consuming."* I then asked about her fees. She said, *"Oh, I don't charge because I don't believe the school will want to pay my fees. Therefore, I volunteer and work with the children at no cost."*

- So many people are afraid to charge what their services are really worth.

- It bothers me to see people who do not understand the value of their self-worth.

- If you are not charging what you are worth out of fear that no one will be willing to pay your price......*check your self-confidence*!

God has not given us a spirit of fear!

But of POWER, LOVE and a SOUND MIND.

2 Timothy 1:7 (NKJV)

If you are a coach, for example, it must have cost you a certain amount of money to acquire those skills and knowledge.

_____

_____

_____

_____

The value you offer to your clients *MUST* be way higher than what you are charging.

_____

_____

_____

_____

You must be willing to invest in yourself; you are your biggest asset.

_____

_____

_____

Learn how to monetize your service or product, and solicit feedback from your clients and others.

_____

_____

_____

Become a subject matter expert in your field.

_____

_____

_____

_____

If you are in business to grow your net-worth, having low self-worth will defeat the purpose of building wealth through your business.

_____

_____

_____

_____

_____

_____

Self-worth versus net-worth.

_____

_____

_____

_____

_____

_____

_____

NET-WORTH = ASSETS minus LIABILITIES

NET-WORTH = WHAT IS OWNED minus

WHAT IS OWED

SELF-WORTH = THE OPINION YOU HAVE ABOUT YOURSELF plus

THE VALUE YOU PLACE ON YOURSELF.

_____

_____

_____

_____

_____

_____

_____

_____

_____

_____

Some people have a very high net-worth, but their self-worth is very low.

_____

_____

_____

_____

_____

_____

People who have a high self-worth are motivated and happy.

_____

_____

_____

_____

_____

_____

"I praise you because I am fearfully and wonderfully made; your works are wonderful, I know that full well." — Psalm 139:14 (NKJV)

"You can be the most beautiful person in the world and everybody sees light and rainbows when they look at you, but if you yourself don't know it, all of that doesn't even matter. Every second that you spend on doubting your worth, every moment that you use to criticize

yourself; is a second of your life wasted, is a moment of your life thrown away. It's not like you have forever, so don't waste any of your seconds, don't throw even one of your moments away."

— C. JoyBell C.

Chapter 2

LEARN TO

ACCEPT YOURSELF

Y ou may be surprised at how many people lack the ability to accept themselves for who they are. Many people are able to put on a front so they appear self-confident when they really are not. The good news is even if you are one of these people, you can learn how to accept yourself. If you are suffering from low self-worth and self-confidence**,** you really do have the ability to turn things around.

I can do all things through Christ who gives me strength.

— Philippians 4:13 (NKJV)

Accepting yourself can mean the difference between a life of happiness and a life of

sadness.

_____

_____

_____

_____

_____

_____

_____

_____

_____

_____

_____

_____

_____

7 Steps to Self-Acceptance:

There are many methods and tips that you'll encounter on your way to acceptance as you find your own unique way of getting there.

Here are a few I have found to be foundational.

1. **Allow for Mistakes:**

_____

_____

_____

_____

_____

2. Live in the Present:

_____

_____

_____

_____

_____

3. **Avoid Comparing Yourself to Others:**

_____

_____

_____

_____

_____

_____

4. **Set Realistic and Relevant Goals:**

_____

_____

_____

_____

_____

_____

5. **Be accepting of yourself:**

_____

_____

_____

_____

_____

_____

6. **Think Positive Thoughts:**

_____

_____

_____

_____

_____

_____

"I *AM* good enough and there *IS* more

for me to learn."

"There *IS* more than enough for everyone.

"I love myself and I *AM* lovable!"

7. Help From Your Loved Ones:

_____

_____

_____

_____

_____

_____

_____

Self-Love:

_____

_____

_____

_____

_____

We form the reality of who we are based on the beliefs we grew up with. It is time to challenge those beliefs.

_____

_____

_____

_____

_____

_____

_____

Daily Affirmations:

- **Get in the habit of repeating daily affirmations about what you want for your life and how you want to be seen by others and yourself.**

- **Write them out and repeat several times during the day until it becomes programmed into your brain. Remember to make it real, because your brain believes what it feels.**

_____

_____

_____

_____

_____

_____

_____

_____

"Your subconscious mind

will act to the given instructions

that are emotionalized and

handed over to it with feelings."

– Napoleon Hill

DAILY AFFIRMATIONS:

I am good enough. I approve of and love myself. I am loved: I accept who I am.

I expect good things to happen to me.

Loving people are always attracted to me. I give myself permission to love me

just as I am. Every day in every way I am getting better and better. I am

fearfully and wonderfully made in God's image.

Our thoughts are very powerful.

_____

_____

_____

_____

_____

_____

_____

Waiting in expectancy—is to be in a spirit of gratitude.

_____

_____

_____

_____

_____

_____

When you begin to change the way you see yourself, you will experience a real change in your life.

_____

_____

_____

_____

_____

_____

_____

Nothing is given to man on earth – struggle is built into the nature of life, and conflict is possible – the hero/heroine is the man/woman who lets no obstacle prevent him/her from pursuing the values he/she has chosen.

– Andrew Bernstein

Chapter 3

BUILDING
SELF-CONFIDENCE

t is said that inside of every woman is a little girl who stands guard at her heart in order to protect it. For some, this little girl has been there for so long that it has become the norm. It is time to go within and find that little girl, so that the little girl might grow up. It's time to tell her that it is safe to come out; it is safe to open up her mind to change and growth. It is time to reactivate dreams that have been deferred as well as aborted. As well, it is time to refresh those dreams that are stuck.

Women are very influential beings, and unfortunately, some women have lost that influence.

_____

_____

_____

_____

_____

_____

Breathing Exercise

Let me encourage you to stop right now and take a few deep breath and release it slowly.

What I want you to do is breathe in confidence and breathe out insecurity. Breathe in possibility and breathe out hopelessness. Breathe in faith and breathe out fear.

BOLDLY DECLARE WHO YOU ARE.

Affirmation:

I am limitless; I am awesome; I am a unique individual.

I am confident and I love myself.

Building Confidence

_____

_____

_____

_____

_____

_____

_____

Habit of a Confident Woman: Power Pose

_____

_____

_____

_____

_____

_____

_____

Exercise:

Wonder Woman Pose : For a morning routine stand in your power pose for two minutes, with eyes closed, and visualize your day. See yourself accomplishing all that you have to do, breathe in deeply for a count of 3, hold for 1, then breathe out fully for a count of 5. This exercise can boost your day; pre-paving it by visualizing, doing the breathing exercises and power posing. All the while, allowing you to have a relaxed, stress-free and confident day.

Being confident involves both your mind and body.

_____

_____

_____

_____

_____

_____

Being able to stand up at networking events and give your 30 second commercial can definitely boost your self-confidence.

_____

_____

_____

_____

_____

_____

Exercise:

- Write an attention grabbing commercial of yourself highlighting your 'WHY.'

- "Why" describes what you do. Practice it by saying it aloud. Look in the mirror or have a loved one critique you.

- This will help you to perfect your "why" and make it powerful when you do stand up and deliver it.

I have found this formula to be helpful: "I help people_____ (list what you help them DO) so they can HAVE_____ (list what you help them get)." Fill in the blanks and create your elevator pitch. Go out and speak what you are seeking. Learn to lead from within.

I will give thanks to you, for I am fearfully and wonderfully made; wonderful are your works and my soul knows it very well. –Psalm 139:14(ASV)

7 Ways to Raise Your Self-Worth

Having a sense of self-worth and an opinion of yourself without grandiosity is important to be able to live a life of success. Some people need others to validate them. They sometimes base their self-worth on the material things they possess in order to feel good. All that really matter is how you feel about yourself. Once you find it within you to build your self-worth, your life will take a different trajectory.

1.   **Do things you Enjoy**:

_____

_____

_____

_____

2. **Relive Happy moments**:

_____

_____

_____

_____

3. Journaling:

_____

_____

_____

_____

4. Stop self-sabotaging:

_____

_____

_____

_____

5. Your Self-Worth should not be measured by Others:

_____

_____

_____

_____

6. **Think Positive Thoughts:**

_____

_____

_____

_____

7. **Act "As If":**

_____

_____

_____

_____

Tips to Renew your Ego

What are your Needs:

_____

_____

_____

_____

_____

_____

Relinquish the fear of judgment:

_____

_____

_____

_____

_____

_____

Your Image speaks a lot about You:

_____

_____

_____

_____

_____

_____

Assess your Circle:

_____

_____

_____

_____

_____

_____

By effectively implementing these tips, you will begin to notice a rise in your self-esteem as you begin to build your self-worth. Remember, *you are worth the effort;* the world is awaiting your contribution**!**

Do not allow others to silence the greatness that is inside of you, so learn to live life from your higher self, on your terms.

Chapter 4

SUCCESS MINDSET

Developing a mindset geared towards success also helps to boost your confidence. In order to change the way you think, you have to create awareness around your emotions. Being aware of how you feel—whether it is anxious, fearful, sad, or hopeless—is very important in changing the way you think. These are all limiting beliefs or emotions. The ability to control your emotions allows you to cultivate a calm demeanor to communicate with confidence.

Your individual views of the world were formed based on the environment you grew up in; what you saw, heard, were told and experienced. This is the reality you were born into.

_____

_____

_____

_____

_____

Train yourself to become aware of your thoughts and begin functioning from your higher self.

_____

_____

_____

_____

Affirmations:

I am beautiful. I am worth loving. I accept myself.

I trust my inner wisdom. I open new possibilities to my life. I give myself permission to release all fear and doubt. I allow myself to accept my uniqueness. I am limitless. I am successful. I am all-knowing and powerful. I am at peace with my age and my body. I stand in my own power and create my own reality.

Exercise:

- As you repeat these affirmations; you must add emotions and feelings to them.

- Post them in obvious places like your bathroom mirror, your refrigerator, and your desk... even in your purse.

- Repeat them first thing in the morning, during the day, and the last thing before you go to bed.

- The more you affirm a thought, the more your mind will accept it.

- If during the day you feel your confidence begins to slip or if you begin to waver, look at your affirmations and focus on them for a while.

- Take a break, close your door or go to the bathroom and recharge. Whether it is deep breathing, your power pose, or repeating your affirmations, make it a habit to recharge your energy at some point during the day.

- As you repeat these affirmations; you must add emotions and feelings to them.

Speaking negatively about yourself and others can be very toxic and causes you to feel less empowered.

_____

_____

_____

_____

_____

_____

_____

_____

When people do not feel good about themselves; they have a propensity to project what they feel upon others.

_____

_____

_____

_____

_____

_____

Develop a positive mindset:

_____

_____

_____

_____

_____

Six Signs of Self-doubt?

When you are experiencing self-doubt, you can feel defeated. If you find yourself being pulled into negative thoughts from past experiences, focus on positive thoughts. Conversely, when you begin feeling good about yourself, your self-esteem increases and you are more likely to experience great success in every area of your life. When you are no longer experiencing self-doubt, you will live a happier more fulfilling life; build stronger relationships, and be respected more by others. Anyone who is consistently experiencing self-doubt is living beneath their potential.

1. **Being too Sensitive:**

   _____

   _____

   _____

   _____

   _____

   _____

   _____

People who are experiencing self-doubt find it challenging to spend time in silence; therefore, they are frequently wanting to be in the company of others and sometimes even dominating the conversation.

2.   **Fear of Being Alone:**

_____

_____

_____

_____

_____

_____

_____

3. **Fear of Failure:**

_____

_____

_____

_____

_____

_____

4. **False Sense of Humor:**

_____

_____

_____

_____

_____

_____

5. **Inability to give Yourself Credit:**

_____

_____

_____

_____

_____

_____

6. **Indecisiveness:**

_____

_____

_____

_____

_____

_____

_____

Chapter 5

ARE YOU LIVING LIFE BY DEFAULT?

lived life by default for a long time, being unaware of it. My confidence was low and I did not feel good about myself. The bad thing is no one knew. I was doing all that I needed to do, but deep down, I was afraid and did not feel that I was good enough.

I had gone through a divorce, and I remembered the last words I heard from my ex-husband, "You will never make it without me!" I actually started to believe it. I felt unfulfilled and my children were all that I lived for. I was unhappy with my job; even though I was paid well. I was not functioning in my purpose. I had great friends and a strong family support system, but deep down, I knew something was missing. It was just not the life I wanted for myself. I had a rumble in my belly and I needed to bring it out and turn it into a roar, and be the voice for those women who have no voice.

Are you living life by default.

_____

_____

_____

_____

_____

_____

When you spend time thinking about what you want and concentrate on being grateful and appreciative, you will operate at a much higher frequency of knowing; you are in a state of allowing; aligned with the essence of your goals.

_____

_____

_____

_____

_____

_____

The moment I made this mindset shift and began focusing on what *I wanted;* and changed the way *I looked at things*, things actually began to shift in my life.

_____

_____

_____

_____

_____

_____

I understood how to love unconditionally, because I had learned to love myself.

_____

_____

_____

_____

_____

_____

I had value and my talents, gifts and abilities they were unique to me, and no one has

my thumb print.

_____

_____

_____

_____

_____

_____

I believed I was born to empower and inspire other women. My talent was given to me

to help others achieve their own outcome.

_____

_____

_____

_____

_____

Chapter 6

LIVING IN THE MOMENT

Life can be brutal as we get caught up in the daily stressors. We all sometimes forget how to stop and "smell the roses." We forget how to laugh out loud and enjoy the moment. We are so busy at times, trying to be everything to everyone else this is especially true for women. This is what I call the "Superwoman Syndrome." We spend a great amount of time taking care and nurturing others that we forget how to be there for ourselves. Have you tried going to dinner or breakfast alone just enjoying your own company? For some women this will take a lot of courage, but it will help to build your self-confidence. Learn to enjoy your own company and feel good about it. I coached a client who did not feel good about herself. One of her assignments was to go to the movies or go to dinner alone. At first, she was petrified! Finally, she gathered up enough courage to go. She later called me and told me how empowered she felt. All it took was the will for her to say, "I can do this!"

_____

_____

_____

_____

_____

_____

_____

We all must learn how to celebrate what is going right in our lives, and learn from what may be going wrong."

_____

_____

_____

_____

_____

_____

Exercise:

Every morning or every night, list five things you are grateful for. It could be your family, employment, your business, good health, your home, your car, food, clothing, nature, being able to see a beautiful sunset or perhaps, just for being alive.

Live in the moment—and in a state of awareness.

_____

_____

_____

_____

_____

There is an internal dialogue going on in your head.

_____

_____

_____

_____

I am exactly where I need to be at this

present moment. My mind is at peace, this moment is

exactly as it should be.

Stop worrying about what others think of us or what you perceive they are saying.

_____

_____

_____

_____

_____

_____

_____

_____

We have to listen to our bodies.

_____

_____

_____

_____

_____

_____

Carrying emotional baggage:

_____

_____

_____

_____

_____

_____

_____

Your lifestyle is connected to your belief system that is connected to your heart.

_____

_____

_____

_____

_____

_____

Ask yourself, "Am I living in my purpose?" If you don't know, then ask God, or tap into infinite intelligence wait in silence, and the answer will come.

And so I tell you keep on asking and you will receive what you ask for.

Keep on seeking, and you will find. Keep on knocking, and the door will be

opened to you. Luke 11:9 (NLT)

When you are living in your purpose, you tend to feel more confident and life has more meaning.

Chapter 7

The Power of the Mind

Ann Marie Kappel, MBA, Ph.D

77

When the student is ready the teacher will appear. Always remember preparation will always be met with opportunity. You need to expand and elevate your mind if you are serious about improving or changing your situation. If you are seeking good success; you have to obtain knowledge. Reading is one way to do so; therefore, I encourage you to invest in your mind and yourself.

_____

_____

_____

_____

_____

_____

As you acquire this knowledge through reading and expanding the mind; I want you to keep in mind this knowledge will have no value unless it is organized and put to good use for a specific purpose or towards some worthy end.

_____

_____

_____

_____

Form good habits of daily routines. Successful people have daily habits.

_____

_____

_____

_____

*Remember, success and failure is largely results of **HABIT**.*

Tip: It is not the quantity of books that you read but the principles learned that you MASTER!

List of recommended reading:

- ❖ Secret of a Millionaire Mind

- ❖ Think and Grow Rich

- ❖ The Science of Getting Rich

- ❖ The Charge

- ❖ Law of Attraction

- ❖ The Hero's Journey

- ❖ From Trash Man to Cash Man

- ❖ Mindset

- ❖ The Speed of Trust

- ❖ Switch On Your Brain

- ❖ You Can Heal Your Life

- ❖ Mindsight

- ❖ Lean In

- ❖ Pray and Grow Richer

- ❖ Passing it on

This book of the law shall not depart from your mouth; but you shall meditate on it day and night, that you may observe to do according to all that is written in it. For then you will make your way prosperous and then you will have good success."

-- Joshua 1:8

I can do all things through Christ who strengthens me.

Philippians 4:13 (NKJV)

Chapter 8

POSITIVE SELF-TALK

Yogi Berra once said that ninety percent of the game is mental. While Yogi was referring to baseball, this thought also can be compared to our attitudes. Like the old adage, your attitude determines your altitude. It is true in every area of your life. Just as your thoughts determine your destiny!

A can-do attitude and a healthy dose of self-confidence are some of the greatest components to you succeeding in life.

_____

_____

_____

_____

_____

_____

You Are the Master of Your Fate:

_____

_____

_____

_____

_____

_____

_____

Yes, You Can Do It:

_____

_____

_____

_____

_____

_____

Positive Reinforcement is Optimistic:

_____

_____

_____

_____

_____

_____

Cue the Music!

_____

_____

_____

_____

_____

_____

Detoxing your Mind:

_____

_____

_____

_____

_____

_____

- **Get rid of Negative Emotions:**

  _____

  _____

  _____

  _____

- **Focus on Forgiveness:**

  _____

  _____

  _____

  _____

- **Write your Goals and Dreams:**

  _____

  _____

  _____

  _____

- **Open up to new Ideas:**

_____

_____

_____

_____

- **Enjoy Life:**

_____

_____

_____

_____

Remember, *you are your biggest asset and you are very important,* more than those things you clean routinely, and put a lot of emphasis on. Use these tips to detoxify your mind. Also, eliminate stress, worry, self-doubt and negative emotions from your life, so you can enjoy your new beginning.

Chapter 9

EXPANDING YOUR MIND AND DISCOVERING YOUR CORE VALUES

An effective method of identifying your values is to imagine your future. First you want to take the time to assess your life and reflect on different areas of it. After you do this, ask yourself these questions. Where do you see yourself as you get older? What are the things that are most important to you? What do you hope to accomplish in life? Answering these questions will help you discover your values. For instance, if you picture yourself growing old while being close to your family and spending valuable time with your grandkids, then a strong sense of family is one of your core values. You can have many values in life; you just need to discover which ones are your highest priorities. That way, at the end of each day, you can feel confident that you're nurturing the most important parts of your life.

Core Values

There are certain values that most people feel are important. You might find that they're significant to you, too, as part of your core beliefs. You can be a positive influence on others when your core values are aligned with the life you live.

- **Discovering your Personal set of Values.**

  _____

  _____

  _____

  _____

- **Your Values are simply the things that are most important to your very core.**

  _____

  _____

  _____

  _____

Exercise:

Complete the exercise on the next page to determine your core values based on this list. However, you can create your own list. This is just an example.

Select 10 core values from the list, next select five from the 10 and finally select the top 3 from the 5.

Arts	Independence
Advancement and Promotion	Influence
Affection	Freedom
Achievement	Friendship
Change	Growth
Close relationships	Loyalty
Community	Wealth
Competence	Personal Development
Decisiveness	Status
Excellence	Independence

- **Beautiful Inside and Out:**

  _____

  _____

  _____

  _____

- **List what you Love about You:**

  _____

  _____

  _____

  _____

- **Avoid Negativity:**

  _____

  _____

  _____

  _____

Being Authentic

_____

_____

_____

_____

_____

_____

_____

Ask yourself, "Am I being me or a carbon copy of someone else?" You are authentically you when you become the best expression of your truth, your feelings and your impulses, and you do this in every moment.

As you begin to be honest with yourself, life will get easier.

_____

_____

_____

_____

_____

_____

I strongly encourage you to believe and keep thinking that you can do and be everything you desire, even if it seems impossible at the moment. Set your intentions, dream big dreams, set audacious goals, and then let it go. All you need to be concerned with is the 'Why' and the 'What.' Let God, the Universe, Spirit, Source—or whatever your higher power is—take care of the 'How.'

Chapter 10

APPRECIATION & GRATITUDE

Learning to appreciate the small things in life can be very meaningful. I encourage you to get a gratitude journal, and each morning, before you begin your day, list about five things you are grateful for. As you begin to list things, you will notice your attitude will begin to change. All you need to do is take a few moments, each day, and express gratitude to your higher power. For me this is God.

When you show gratitude; it opens up a flood gate of blessings for you. It will begin to attract more things into your life.

_____

_____

_____

_____

_____

Learn to have an attitude of gratitude.

_____

_____

_____

_____

_____

There has been research that shows merely repeating a prayer or affirmation has no real effect on the brain. However, once you fully immerse yourself in the prayer or affirmation, the manner in which the brain responds can transform a person's life.

_____

_____

_____

_____

_____

Exercise:

Add emotions and feelings to your affirmation.

First, write down all of your best qualities. Next, think about what others would add to your board. Finally, call up some colleagues and friends who know you well and ask them what your strengths are. Once you begin listing them; you will begin to feel so good and what you perceive to be weaknesses will no longer bother you.

This is for all the phenomenal women out there in this vast Universe.

"I'M A WOMAN PHENOMENALLY.

PHENOMENAL WOMAN,

THAT'S ME"

– Dr. Maya Angelou

Afterword

In this book the importance of having a positive mindset and being aware of your thoughts were addressed. When you are seeking change, one thing you must understand is you cannot use the same mindset that caused a problem in your life to find the solution. Therefore, you must be transformed by the renewing of your mind. There are 3C's to remember. If you want anything in life to Change, you must make the Choice to take the Chance in order to make it happen.

I encourage you to live a life of grace. Amazing grace! The most perfect life is a life lived in grace. The good thing about grace is that it is available to all; it meets us where we are. When you learn to give freely it is given under grace. Learn to desire grace for others. Connect with the grace of God and let it flow through you.

When you allow your deepest desires to come alive and flow from you, you open your heart to everything that is possible. My desire is that you have allowed your heart to be open while reading this book to awaken the qualities of your true self, and ultimately, finding out who you really are and why you are here.

Become the change you want to see.

– Mahatma Gandhi.

Allow your presence to uplift and enlighten others by becoming the spark that encourages others to grow, live and prosper. Allow spiritual and material abundance to radiate from you. As you continue along this journey, like a child who is learning to walk; you will fall down sometimes. The practice of falling down will give you the resilience, the tenacity and perseverance to get better, if you do not allow yourself to get bitter in life.

I am Dr. Ann M. Kappel and with the following, I want to EMPOWER "U" with words that you can repeat aloud.

I choose to love myself and to love others

I choose to renew my mind

I choose to be my authentic self

I choose to be happy

I choose success and abundance

I choose to love my life

I choose to change

I choose to live more deeply

I choose resilience over resentment

I choose Faith over fear

I choose to forgive

I choose to be motivated

I choose abundance over lack

I choose to be Empowered and stand in my Power!

I am grateful for the gift of Choice………

In Gratitude,
Dr. K.

CALL TO ACTION

Simple Exercises to a Mindset Shift

I am now free to love myself:

Learning to love yourself; who am I?

List 3-5 things you like about yourself

List 3-5 things you will forgive yourself for

List 2 people you will forgive. Call them or write a letter; if they are deceased, shred

or burn the letter to bring closure.

List 3-5 things you will no longer criticize about your self

List 1-3 things you want to change to improve your life

Write out and repeat 7 times, "I love and accept myself, I am willing to change. I give myself permission to accept all possibilities into my life"

Self-Worth:

I free myself to be ME by creating my own Reality:

List 1-3 limiting beliefs you will release

List one challenge you will take that you were once fearful of doing

List 1-3 things you desire to have that will change your future

Write out the steps necessary to accomplish the things you desire to change. They must be specific, clear, concise and achievable.

(List the date you desire to have it, the amount - if it is money, the size if it is weight loss). List what you will give in return for what you desire? Keep it before you daily. As you think about it add emotions. See yourself already having it.

List your proudest accomplishment or win

List one of your most meaningful moments

List 1 talent or skill you possess

What is your passion?

Do you know your purpose? Go within and find what makes you happy when you do it. It may be as simple as making the lives of others better.

What is Your Purpose? Write it out.

Daily Visioning:

I open New doors to My life:

Value yourself on a scale of 1-10 and imagine what life will look like if you were a perfect "10" in any area of your life (finance, health, relationship, or spirituality). Now picture in your mind's eye the type of day you will have as a perfect "10" and see it unfolding for you. Practice this before you start your day.

Know your "*WHY*"

**(*The purpose, belief or cause that inspires you to do what you do).*

People are so much in the habit of asking **HOW** can I make this happen for me? When you have a dream yet to be fulfilled; what you should ask is: **WHY** do I want this? I believe two of the most important days in a person's life is the day he/she was born and the day you discover **WHY** you were born.

Steps to your WHY:

Get clear on your WHY

Become emotionally involved with your WHY

Once you are clear and emotionally involved, ideas, the right people, resources and opportunities will begin to show up for you. Ultimately your dreams will become realities.

This only happens when you are clear about your WHY.

My Why is.......

As I move into the winning circle, I am living a life of integrity, authenticity and significance. Everything I touch is a success. Every day in every way I am getting better, better, better. All is well in my world. Everything is working out for my highest good.

I greet each day with gratitude; with open arms I say, Thank You! Namaste.

Resources

The Bible – New King James Translation

The Bible – New Living Translation

The Bible – American Standard Version

Bernstein, A. BrainyQuote. www.brainyquote.com/qotes/authors

Breathnach, S. (2009). *Simple abundance: a daybook of comfort and joy*. New York: Grand Central Publishing.

Hill, N. – (1937) Think and Grow Rich.

Morrissey, M., (2012) – Dream Builder Live

Myths of Retirement – http://iwc.tiaa-cref.org/private/participants/appmanager

Serendipity's guide to savings. Women Money Week. www.savernot aspendet.blogspot.com/

Workshop: Healing the daughters of Narcissistic Mothers Virtual Workshop. http://www.willieverbegoodenough.com/workshop-overview-healing-the-daughters-of-narcissistic-mothers

The state of women owned business. http//:www.womenable.com/contentuserfee2014

US Census Bureau, Numbers, timing and duration of marriage and divorce.

www.census.gov/pool/2011pubs/p70-125pdf.

Waldman, M. (2015) – www.markrobertWaldman.com

About the Author

Dr. Ann Marie Kappel is purpose-driven and committed to empowering women to unapologetically live their best life now being authentically you. She believes women should stand in their power, be present, and show up for life. Dr. Kappel is the CEO of Alpha Consulting & Empowerment and the founder of Life Transformation & Connections, an organization for women *"where real change happens."* She masterfully integrates her extensive education as a Psychologist and Master Neuro Linguistic Practitioner and her many years of corporate experience to impact the lives of those she comes in contact with. Through her compassion, enthusiasm, and passion, she helps her clients develop a mind-set geared for success while identifying their life purpose by applying her transformational emotional wellness principles.

As an Executive Coach, she specializes in empowering leaders to strive to be their best selves, and achieve self-empowerment through personal growth and development. Dr. Kappel works with women coaching them to increase their net-worth and build their self-worth. She also coaches adolescents as early as age 13, who are not sure what they desire to pursue in college, feel stressed, have self-esteem or self-confidence issues and are seeking to improve their lives by way of personal growth and development.

Dr. Kappel is also an Adjunct Professor, Certified Score Business Mentor and Speaker. She coauthored Customer Service and Professionalism for Women and is the Author of her Signature Coaching Program, "The Empowered Woman: Twenty-One-Day Intensive" and her E-book, "The Empowered Woman."

Dr. Kappel will help you go within, unlock your genius and make a mindset shift in order to live life on purpose doing what you love.

For more information,

Visit: www.drannkappel.com

www.ingramcontent.com/pod-product-compliance
Lightning Source LLC
Chambersburg PA
CBHW081147040426
42445CB00015B/1799